Exploring Earth and Space

Exploring Rocks and Minerals

Greg Roza

PowerKiDS press™

NEW YORK

Published in 2013 by The Rosen Publishing Group, Inc.
29 East 21st Street, New York, NY 10010

Book Design: Michael Harmon

Photo Credits: Cover LVV/Shutterstock.com; p. 4 Andrea Danti/Shutterstock.com; pp. 5, 21 iStockphoto/Thinkstock.com; pp. 6 (volcanic rock), 7 © iStockphoto.com/prill; pp. 6 (layered rock), 8 Thinkstock/Thinkstock.com; pp. 6 (marbled rock), 9LesPalenik/Shutterstock.com; pp. 10, 12, 20 Hemera/Thinkstock.com; p. 13 Oleg - F/Shutterstock.com; p. 14 (copper ore) Terry Davis/Shutterstock.com; p. 14 (zinc) © iStockphoto.com/bagi1998; p. 15 Bruno Morandi/The Image Bank/Getty Images; p. 16 George Doyle/Thinkstock.com; p. 17 D. Anschutz/Thinkstock.com; p. 18 Kiransov/Shutterstock.com; p. 19 Ed Lallo/Photolibrary/Getty Images; p. 22 Noel Hendrickson/Thinkstock.com.

Library of Congress Cataloging-in-Publication Data

Roza, Greg.
Exploring rocks and minerals / Greg Roza.
    p. cm.— (Exploring Earth and space)
Includes index.
ISBN: 978-1-4488-8830-6
6-pack ISBN: 978-1-4488-8831-3
ISBN: 978-1-4488-8576-3 (lib. bdg.)
1. Rocks—Juvenile literature. 2. Minerals—Juvenile literature. I. Title.
QE432.2.R69 2013
552—dc23

2012010153

Manufactured in the United States of America

CPSIA Compliance Information: Batch #WS12RC: For further information contact Rosen Publishing, New York, New York at 1-800-237-9932.

Word Count: 451

Contents

All About Earth

Earth is a big place. It's really old, too. Do you know what Earth is made of?

Earth is made of rocks and minerals. We see rocks and minerals almost every day. Some rocks are really big. Other rocks are small.

Kinds of Rocks

Rocks are hard things we find outside. We can't make them, but Earth can. There are three kinds of rocks.

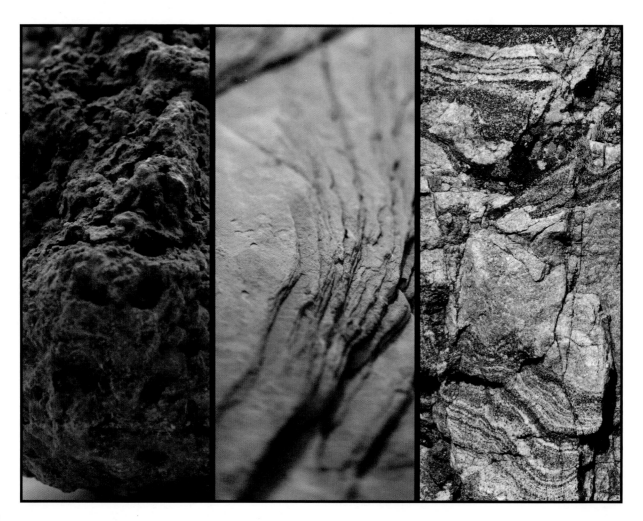

One kind of rock is made from **lava**. Lava is a hot **liquid**. Earth makes it under the ground. When lava comes out of the ground, it cools and becomes hard.

Earth makes another kind of rock by pressing mud and sand together. They mix together and become hard. Then the mix becomes a rock. This takes a very long time.

The third kind of rock is made by changing rocks that are already here. How does that happen? Sometimes Earth presses so hard on rocks that it changes them!

Fossils

Sometimes, plants and animals get stuck in rocks! They leave remains called a **fossil**. Have you ever seen a fossil? They're really old!

Finding Fossils

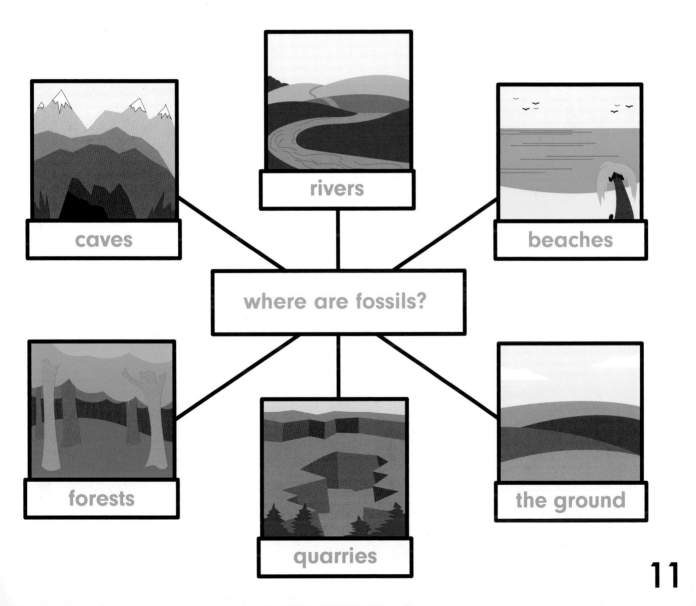

caves

rivers

beaches

where are fossils?

forests

quarries

the ground

Minerals

All rocks are different. They can be different sizes and shapes. All rocks are made of minerals. Some rocks are made of many different minerals.

Minerals aren't living things. We can't make minerals.
We find them by digging in the ground. There are many
kinds of minerals on Earth.

All minerals are different. They can be hard or they can be soft. Some minerals have beautiful colors. Other minerals are very **shiny**.

We can do different tests to find out what a mineral is.

We look at their colors. We smell them, too.

Some minerals smell really bad!

Our bodies need some minerals to stay healthy. Do
you know why we drink milk? Milk has a mineral called
calcium. Calcium gives us strong bones and teeth.

Our bodies also need iron. It's a mineral that makes us stronger. We have iron in our blood. We get iron when we eat vegetables.

Using Rocks and Minerals

A lot of people study Earth for their jobs. They use rocks and minerals to learn about Earth. It helps us understand where we live.

We learn about Earth in school, too. Sometimes your teacher will bring in rocks and minerals. You get to hold them and look at them.

We use rocks to make buildings. The rocks make the
buildings strong. The rocks keep the buildings safe from
bad weather. They also make the buildings pretty.

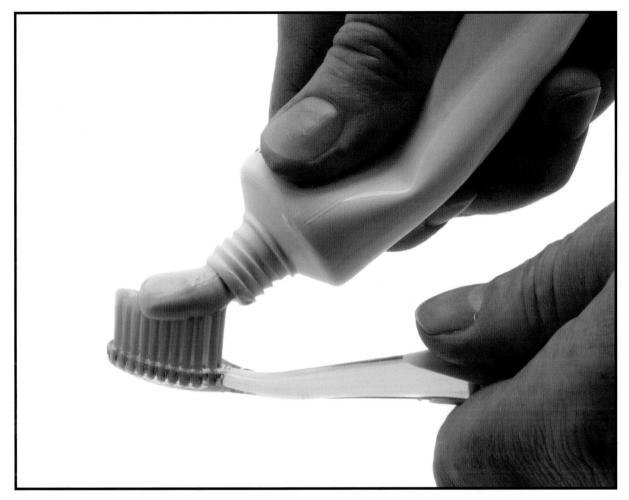

We use some minerals every day. There's one kind
of mineral in our toothpaste. It gives us beautiful and
healthy teeth!

Sometimes, people climb on rocks. They climb high into the air. It can be hard, but it's good exercise. Some people think this is a lot of fun!

Glossary

calcium (KAL-see-uhm) A mineral that makes bones and teeth strong.

fossil (FAH-suhl) Remains of an animal or plant in a rock.

lava (LAH-vuh) Hot, liquid rock that comes out of Earth.

liquid (LIH-kwuhd) Something that flows like water.

shiny (SHY-nee) Bright or giving off a bright light.

Index

Due to the changing nature of Internet links, The Rosen Publishing Group, Inc., has developed an online list of websites related to the subject of this book. This site is updated regularly. Please use this link to access the list: **www.powerkidslinks.com/ees/rock**